Geography Junction

Weather
Activity Book

GW00786788

Contents

Introduction

This activity book has been produced to provide a range of weather activities for primary school children. It is divided into six sections, each one serving as a starting-point for a weather project. Each section looks at different aspects of weather, some of which link strongly to other curriculum areas, such as maths, science and English.

Each unit is introduced by a page of Teachers' Notes which gives:
* background information;
* ways of using each activity sheet;
* a display idea.

The activity sheets

Geography
The 30 activity sheets offer a range of learning objectives, giving opportunities for the following geographical skills:
* observation;
* use of recording instruments;
* use of thematic maps;
* fieldwork in the school grounds;
* use of appropriate geographical vocabulary;
* use of a questionnaire;
* use of secondary sources, e.g. newspapers.

Within a thematic study of weather children can study:
* how site conditions influence weather;
* seasonal weather patterns;
* weather conditions in different parts of the world.

Science
In experimental and investigative science, collecting and recording weather records, making simple apparatus, and observing and testing the effects of the weather, all give opportunities for children to:
* plan experimental work;
* obtain evidence;
* consider evidence.

In addition, the weather activities give a wealth of opportunity for:
* systematic enquiry;
* experience of scientific ideas;
* communication by scientific methods.

Maths
There are many opportunities for children to use and apply their mathematical knowledge in real situations when studying the weather. Different activity sheets give the opportunity to practise:
* measuring volume;
* reading scales;
* calculating averages;
* observing patterns;
* collecting data;
* interpreting tables.

English
Children are asked to write in response to a variety of tasks.
In this set of activity sheets there are opportunities for:
* extending vocabulary;
* developing and communicating ideas;
* discussion;
* use of information from a range of sources.

Information and computer technology
The study of weather and use of ICT are natural partners. Both encourage enquiry and practical activities. Children collect, record and analyse data. Work on the activity sheets in this book could be extended to include the following:
* entering weather records on a database, e.g. 'Our facts';
* interrogating a database to draw graphs and charts, e.g. 'Our facts – grass';
* making a weather map, e.g. 'Weathermapper';
* collecting data from other sources, e.g. Ceefax, television and news programmes, the Internet;
* using a fax to receive a daily weather chart from Metfax 0336 400487.

FOG

Progression and Differentiation

What to teach

The activity sheets in this book are suitable for primary age children at different stages of learning. Individual children in a class will be at different levels so their work will need to be differentiated. If a weather project takes place in several classes, the geography co-ordinator may like to plan which aspects should be covered in each class, in order to prevent repetition as the child moves through the school.

Progressing the activity sheets

In the 'Weather Recording' unit there is progression through Activities 1–3 on how to use thermometers. The teacher should choose which activity best suits the ability of the child as the starting-point.

Similarly, with Activities 6–8, children will cope with different activities in 'Measuring the Wind'. It is sometimes a good idea to use a range of activity sheets with different groups in a class. Ask each group to present their work to the others so they all gain some experience of the different ways work can be undertaken.

Progressive learning in the 'Effects of Weather' section can follow the order of the activity sheets, which deals firstly with the child's own experiences, moves into the local area and then beyond into different effects of weather around the world.

Special needs

With special needs children you could: pair children to work together on a difficult or lengthy activity; cut up activity sheets and present them as smaller units of work; enlarge maps, diagrams or parts of activity sheets; highlight entries in tables and charts to make them easier for children to focus on; use classroom assistants or more able older children to help with activity sheets that require reading instruments.

When to use the activity sheets

It is not necessary to work through all the activities during a weather topic. 'Weather Recording' may be used over a two-week period in each season. During studies of localities, a range of activities on effects of weather and world weather can be used. Activity sheets that link with other subjects may be used individually to enhance practical activities related to science and maths.

Display

Each unit gives one idea for displaying the activity sheets or work related to the unit. Displaying the children's work enables them to learn from each other, see other approaches, or use an interactive display as a resource.

'Which weather?' quiz (Activity 30)

The answers to expect for each illustration are:

rocks:
* erosion;
* sandstorm;
* particles of sand carried by the wind erode the rock.

soil:
* evaporation;
* sun;
* hot weather evaporates moisture in clay soils, cracking surfaces.

trees:
* prevailing wind;
* wind;
* trees in exposed places grow in a leaning position, away from prevailing wind direction.

cars:
* loss of friction;
* temperature;
* fall in temperature causes ice on roads – cars slide and crash due to loss of friction.

telephone boxes:
* hurricane;
* knock-on effect;
* in 1987, storms caused trees to fall all over southern England.

floods:
* rain;
* burst;
* houses vulnerable to floods when rivers burst their banks often show past flood levels.

FOG

Weather Recording

Recording the weather gives children the opportunity to work outside as fieldwork, and to develop the skills of mapwork, direction finding and recording.

☀ A Stevenson screen is ideal to keep instruments in.

The activity sheets
Activities 1–4
Four progressive activities in temperature reading for children at different ability levels.

Notes:
☀ It is easier to use a thermometer if a strip of paper is laid across the top of the liquid to read the scale.
☀ It is good practice to use °C after each reading. C stands for Celsius; F stands for Fahrenheit, which is seldom used nowadays.
☀ A maximum/minimum thermometer records hottest and coldest temperatures between resetting the instrument. The maximum and minimum temperatures are taken at the pinheads, the present temperature at the liquid levels.
☀ The school grounds will have a microclimate, with temperatures influenced by buildings, materials and the sun's position.

Expected answers on the temperature trail

		Influences on temperature
In a wooden weather box.	1.	Most accurate. Heat reflected and air cooled.
Hanging in a tree.	2.	In the shade and off hot ground.
In a sheltered corner.	3.	Warmth from building but in shade.
On a wall, in the shade.	4.	Coldest. Wind cooled and no sun.
In the school greenhouse.	5.	Hottest. Intensified heat. No air flow.
Floating in a pond.	6.	Deep water cold but sun heats surface.

Groups of children can make and set a temperature trail for others to follow.

5. Make a rain gauge
With young children it may be better to record once a week when there is more rain to record. Stabilise the rain gauge by sinking it in the ground a little.

6. Measure the wind
This wind scale is for comparing wind speeds in your school grounds. The numbers will not relate to any other scale such as the Beaufort Scale.

7. Wind direction
The conical roof, or cowl, of an oasthouse is turned by the wind to help the smoke from fires drying hops to escape. Children may need to be taught that wind direction is where the wind has come from.

8. Take an angle on the wind
Using a protractor and learning how to measure angles can be linked with this activity. As long ago as 1450, Leon Alberti was measuring the wind in Italy by recording how far a ball swung along a curved scale in different winds.

9. The weather this week
The weather chart can be filled with symbols or numbers. Cloud cover can be measured by estimating what fraction of the sky has clouds, usually in ⅛ths.

Display idea
Children can make small cards which show symbols and numbers. Velcro stapled to the back of each one allows them to be fixed to Velcro on the display board. They can be changed daily to match recordings and weather conditions. A master record sheet keeps the whole week's weather on show.

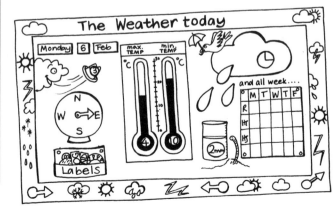

FOG

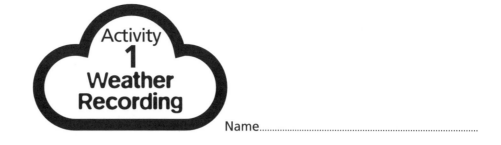

Activity
1
Weather Recording

Name..

Can you read a thermometer?

1. Colour the liquid in each thermometer.
2. Use a ruler to line up the top of the liquid with the scale.
3. Record the temperature in °C.

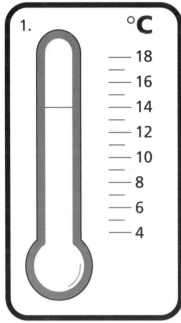

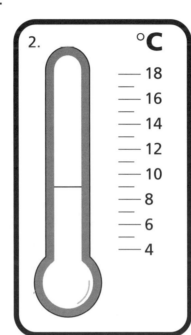

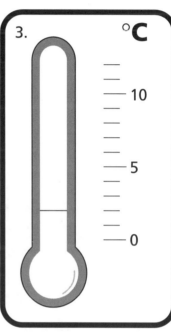

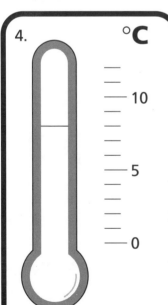

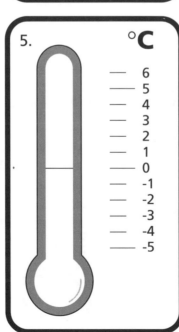

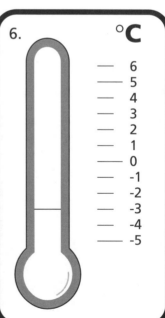

The hottest temperature is_____°C.   The coldest temperature is_____°C.

Name..

Different temperatures

Different places and different things
have different temperatures.
Use a thermometer to find the
temperature of these.

Handy Hints

1. Don't hold the thermometer bulb in
   your hand, it will raise the
   temperature.
2. Give the thermometer a few minutes
   to adjust to each new temperature.
3. A thermometer is fragile – be careful
   with it.

1. The air.

....

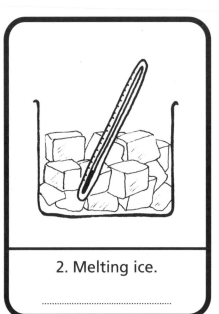

2. Melting ice.

....

3. Against the window.

....

4. Tap water.

....

5. Under your arm.

....

What was the range of
temperatures?
(The difference between
the coldest and the
hottest.)

....

Name...

Using a maximum/minimum thermometer

Can you read three temperatures from this thermometer?
1. The present temperature.
2. The coldest temperature since you last used it.
3. The hottest temperature since you last used it.

Look for these features on the thermometer:
* two floating pins;
* the thermometer liquid;
* the scale;
* the minus numbers on the scale;
* the reset button.

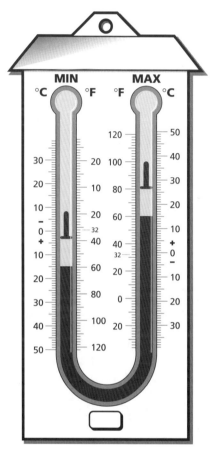

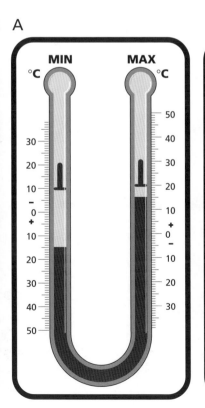

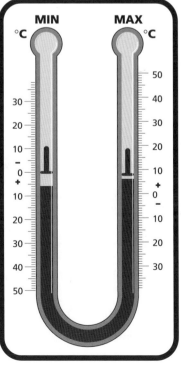

Use these thermometers to practise reading the temperatures.

Record all three temperatures for each thermometer.

A   B

maximum ....   maximum ....

minimum ....   minimum ....

present ....   present ....

How does this thermometer help people to record the weather?
Why is this thermometer particularly useful in greenhouses?

Name..

A temperature trail

There are six thermometers to visit in this trail. Find them on the plan and match the numbers to the place descriptions opposite.

Floating in a pond.	
In a wooden weather box.	
In the school greenhouse.	
In a sheltered corner.	
Hanging in a tree.	
On a wall, in the shade.	

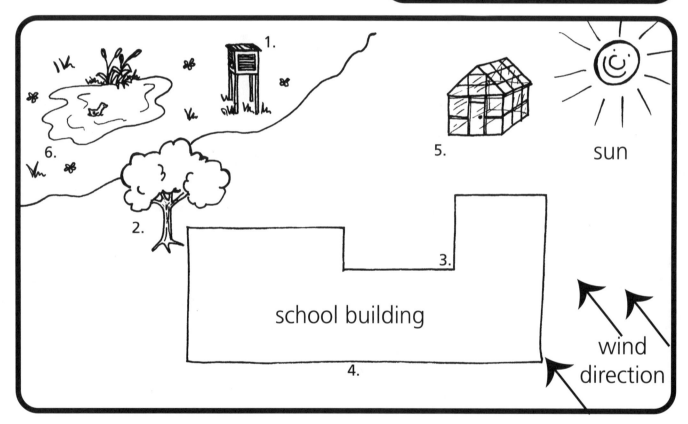

Each temperature was taken at the same time on a sunny but windy day. The temperatures were all slightly different.

✳ Which place was the hottest? Why?
✳ Which place was the coldest? Why?
✳ Which place gave the most accurate temperature? Why do you think that?

Make your own temperature trail. Draw a plan of your school. Where would you place thermometers to make a temperature trail? Try to put them in order, starting with the hottest. Now test your list with a thermometer. Were you right?

Name..

Make a rain gauge

1. Choose a plastic bottle that is smooth and clear.

2. Cut the top from the bottle and turn it over so that it acts as a funnel.

3. The wind may blow your rain gauge over. Think of a way to keep it stable.

4. Fix paper with a scale starting from the base of the bottle to show how much rain has fallen. Waterproof the scale with see-through adhesive.

5. Decide whether to measure rainfall each day or each week. Remember it is hard to measure small amounts of rainwater.

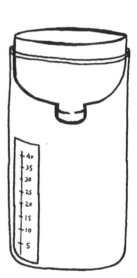

6. Make a chart to record your rainfall measurements.

Name:	Location:
Date	Rainfall
1.2.99	3 mm
8.2.99	0 mm
15.2.99	5 mm

7. Compare your measurements with others. If they are different, why do you think that is?

If it snows, then calculate that 30 cm of snow equals 2.5 cm of rain.

FOG

Measure the wind

Measure the speed of the wind each day with your own wind scale.

1. Take a wire coat hanger and bend it into an L-shape.

2. Attach a piece of card to the lower arm of the hanger so that it will move freely, and is almost touching the ground.

3. Push one arm of your wind scale into a bottle nearly full of water. This heavy base will stop it being blown over.

4. Place a ruler at right angles to the card. This will be your scale. The wind will blow the card and you can read on the ruler the distance in centimetres it has blown.

5. Make a chart to record your readings and compare daily wind speeds over one or two weeks.

Date	How the wind feels	My scale
Jan 6th	Paper blowing around playground	4 cm
~~7~~	~~Paper blowing~~	~~5~~

FOG

Wind direction

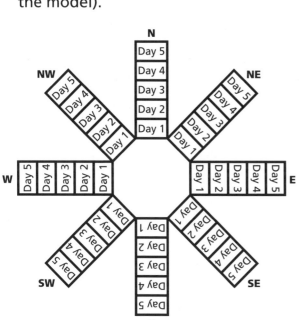

Oasthouses in Kent have a roof which is turned by the wind to let smoke escape. Fires inside dry hops for beer-making. The vane on the roof is pushed around by the wind.

Make your own wind vane. This model oasthouse is one idea you could use.

1. For the base – fill a plastic bottle with sand or water for stability. Cover it and draw brick patterns and a door.

2. For the cowl – paint or cover a narrow tub.

3. For the vane – cut a 2–3 cm wide strip of card twice the height of the tub. Fold it in half. Fold back 2 cm at each end and fix to the tub. Slot in your own emblem and glue the sides of the wind vane together.

4. Record the direction of the wind (where the wind comes from) each day. Remember: the wind which blows the vane around comes from the opposite side of the oasthouse (look at the picture of the model).

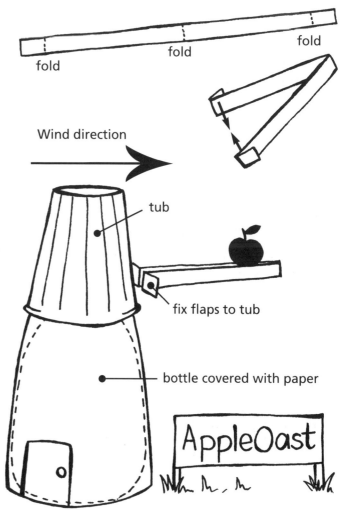

fold   fold   fold

Wind direction

tub

fix flaps to tub

bottle covered with paper

AppleOast

Make a large wind rose to record wind direction. Each day find out the wind direction and colour one section for that day. Start from the centre.
Where does the wind come from most of the time?
Make a chart that shows what the weather is like with each wind direction.

16

FOG

Take an angle on the wind

In 1805, Sir Francis Beaufort, a naval admiral, designed a system for measuring winds at sea by looking at the effect of the wind on waves and sails. His idea was adapted for use on land and is called the Beaufort Scale.

Force 6 – Strong breeze

Describe what is happening in the pictures.

Make a simple ball wind instrument using a table-tennis ball attached to dark-coloured thread.

1. Use a large blackboard protractor or make one from stiff card.

2. Hold the instrument parallel to the wind.

3. Read the angle at which the ball is blown.

4. Use it in different places to see how wind speed is affected by buildings.

5. Make a chart of your findings.

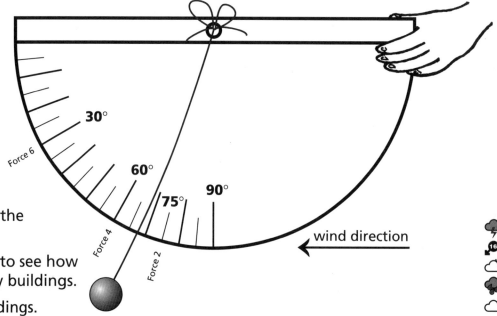

FOG

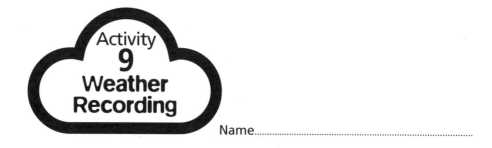

Name...

The weather this week

	Monday	Tuesday	Wednesday	Thursday	Friday
Minimum temperature					
Maximum temperature					
Wind direction					
Wind strength					
Rainfall					
Clouds					

If you don't have a maximum/minimum thermometer, then take the temperature at different times of the day and use the hottest and coldest readings. In the clouds box record how much cloud you can see.

FOG

Weather Lore

Long before weather forecasting was carried out by meteorologists people needed to know what weather to expect. This was vital information for sailors and farmers, so people started to look for signs that would help them predict the weather. Many sayings about the weather cannot be supported scientifically, although they may be true for some geographical locations. Some are merely superstitions.

It is fun for children to look for clues that forecast the weather. Here are two natural items that you could use to forecast rain ahead. Hang them outside for children to observe.

❋ Fir cone – in dry weather the scales open to release the seeds. As the air gets damp, the scales close to keep the seeds inside dry.

❋ Wool – a strand of natural wool shrinks and curls up when dry. When the air is damp, the wool swells and straightens.

The activity sheets

10. Lions and lambs

'March comes in like a lion and goes out like a lamb,' as winter ends and spring begins. Signs of spring include daffodils, snowdrops, birds nesting, hedgehogs emerging and changes in clothes worn. The flow diagram can be extended to produce a concertina book that shows signs of spring: poems, artwork and other March events such as St. David's Day on 1 March.

11. Test a weather forecast

The activity sheet gives a weather prediction for children to test. Decide how often they need to record the weather conditions to check this prediction. Is it fair to base it on one day's weather, or should they watch the weather for a week or more? They can draw their own chart to match the number of days in their test. Use the comments column to record whether the weather saying applies each day.

12. Animal forecasters

Many animals can sense changes in the weather before humans. Often their survival depends on finding food and shelter. It is said that 'raining cats and dogs' refers to medieval times when stray cats and dogs died in street floodings. Left in the gutters, the next day it looked as if it had been raining cats and dogs. A starter sentence could be given for the first box – the children may need further clues. Other sayings include:

❋ Cows are thought to lie down to keep a patch of grass dry when rain is expected.

❋ Folklore says that squirrels grow bushy tails in preparation for a hard winter, but they are more likely to store extra nuts in order to survive.

❋ Grasshoppers make their loud noise by rubbing their back legs against their bodies, perhaps as a cooling device.

None of these sayings have been scientifically proven – they are country lore.

Display idea

Make concertina books as suggested in Activity 10 to suit the season you are in. Mount them on a background of seasonal images. Close the books with a split pin attached to ribbon on the display board. They can be opened for children to read.

16

22

FOG

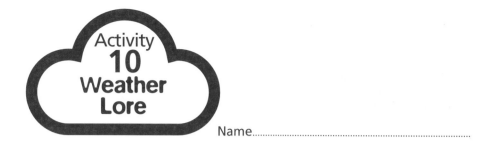
Lions and lambs

There is a saying about the weather in March. It says, 'March comes in like a lion and goes out like a lamb.'

Write some words to describe a lion. ....

Write some words to describe a lamb. ....

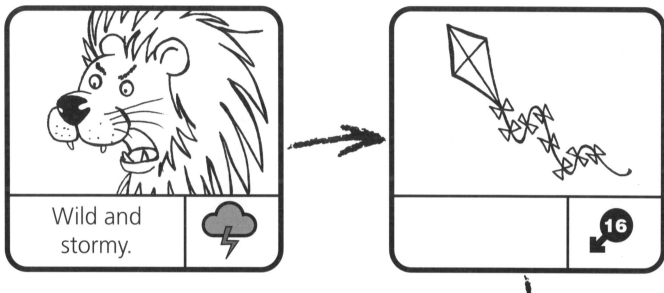

Wild and stormy.

Make a flow diagram by filling in the boxes to show how the weather changes as the month of March proceeds. Fill the empty spaces with symbols, pictures or captions.

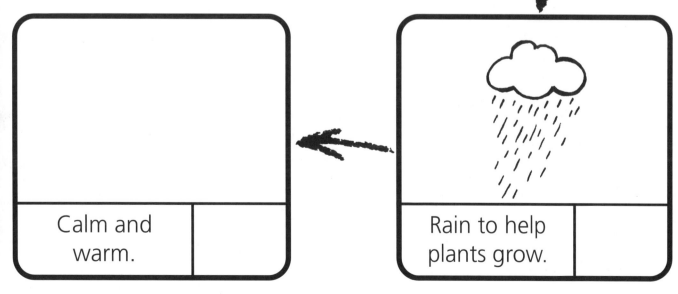

Calm and warm.

Rain to help plants grow.

March is the first month of spring. What signs [o]f spring do you notice where you live?

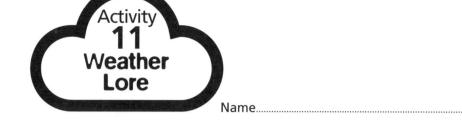

Activity
11
Weather Lore

Name...

Test a weather forecast

**"Twixt twelve and two,
tells what the rest of the day will do.'**

This old saying forecasts the afternoon and evening weather. Can you test if it works? Make a chart like this for the number of days in your test. Each day between midday and two o'clock record the weather. Remember to watch and record the rest of the day's weather as well.

Weather	12 noon – 2 p.m.	Rest of the day	Comments
Monday			
Tuesday			
Wednesday			
Thursday			
Friday			

Use these symbols to record the weather. Match them to the weather description by drawing one in each empty box.

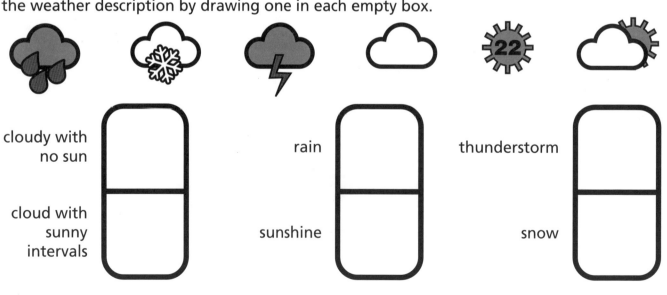

cloudy with
no sun

cloud with
sunny
intervals

rain

sunshine

thunderstorm

snow

Do you think the saying works? How often did it forecast the weather correctly?

FOG

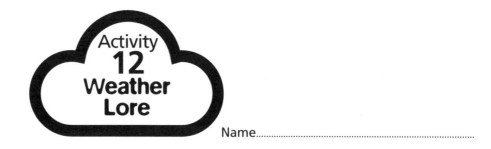
Animal forecasters

Can animals really forecast the weather?

Beside each picture write about that animal and why people think the weather saying may have some meaning.

'It's raining cats and dogs!'

....

....

....

'When cows lie down it's going to rain.'

....

....

....

'Squirrels with bushy tails means a harsh winter to come.'

....

....

....

'Loud grasshoppers means it will be getting hotter.'

....

....

....

Think of another animal. How does it behave when there is a change in the weather?

....

....

FOG

Using the Weather

The sun

We use the sun for heat and light. Plant growth is the easiest way to show this, by growing two plants, one in a dark, cool place and one in a light room and observing the differences. The plant without light cannot produce the chlorophyll that makes plants green. Solar power can be demonstrated with simple solar calculators.

Wind

People have always made use of the wind, from early days, when kites were invented in China, to modern-day harnessing of the wind's energy to provide electricity with aerogenerators. Sailing ships and windmills still rely on the wind, even though technology provides alternative means of power.

Rain

A simple activity can explore children's knowledge by asking them to fill raindrop outlines with different uses of water, using words and pictures. Older children can keep to one area, e.g. agriculture, industry, leisure, at school or in the home.

wash hands   clean buses   provide ice

The activity sheets

13. Telling the time with the sun

The angle of the sundial's triangle is 52°. Able children can draw their own template or change the size of the sundial. Mark a north–south line on the ground in the sun, so that sundials can be quickly positioned outside. Children should notice that the length of the shadows alter during the day, getting shorter towards midday, and longer towards evening. Their marks should show that the sun moves at a uniform rate.

14. Making a kite

The activity sheet shows the actual size of the kite. It can be enlarged for young children. The cross-frame can be made with the dried stems of grasses used for dried arrangements, if you use tissue paper and keep the kite small. Choose a windy day for best results. Explore some wind vocabulary. Ask children to describe the flight of the kites, the sound of the wind, and how the wind feels on their faces.

15. How much water do you use?

Discuss with the children that 70 per cent of the planet is water, but most is salty seawater which we cannot use. We depend on fresh water, pumped from rivers and underground rocks. Shortages occur where there is little rain or the demand for water is very high. This activity can link with a maths project on measuring volume. It will give practice in estimating amounts of liquid, using a tally sheet with ticks or the 5 bar gate system. It can be extended for older children, by making a tally over five days and calculating an average.

Display idea

Make a large kite to hang in the classroom. Along the tail children can add bows with wind words or phrases, discussed during Activity 14, written on them.

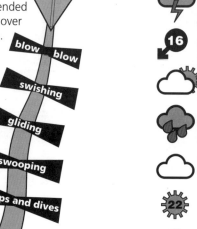

blow   blow
swishing
gliding
swooping
swoops and dives
calms and dies

16

22

FOG

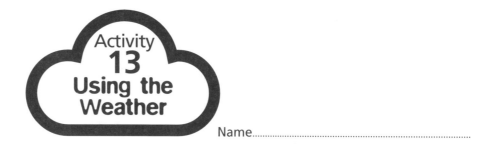

Telling the time with the sun

How to make a sundial:

1. Cut out two cardboard shapes using the template.
2. Fold the flaps out.
3. Glue the triangles together.
4. Draw a semi-circle on a base board.
5. Glue your sundial to the centre of the base.
6. Check it looks like the picture on this page.

How to use the sundial:

1. Place your model on some level ground in the sun.
2. Use a compass to find south.
3. Turn your sundial to point south (check the picture for the right position).
4. On every hour, mark the position of the shadow on the base board.

What do you notice about the shadows you have marked?

Flap to fold outwards

52°

S ←   → **N**

FOG

Making a kite

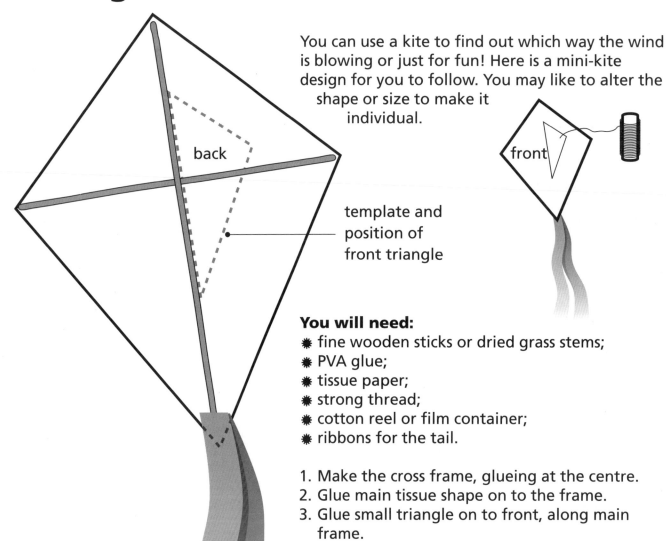

back

You can use a kite to find out which way the wind is blowing or just for fun! Here is a mini-kite design for you to follow. You may like to alter the shape or size to make it individual.

front

template and position of front triangle

You will need:
* fine wooden sticks or dried grass stems;
* PVA glue;
* tissue paper;
* strong thread;
* cotton reel or film container;
* ribbons for the tail.

1. Make the cross frame, glueing at the centre.
2. Glue main tissue shape on to the frame.
3. Glue small triangle on to front, along main frame.
4. Glue one end of a 10–15 m length thread to the small triangle.
5. Wind thread around a reel.
6. Add two 60 cm tails to the back of the kite.

Handy Hints
* make your kite as light as possible – it will fly better;
* allow glue to dry between each stage.

After you have flown your kite, write a report on how it flew. Include any problems you had, and try to describe how the wind acted with the kite.

FOG

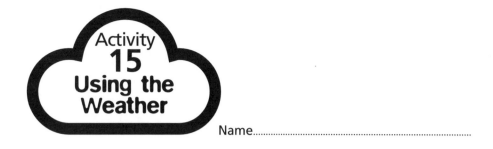

Activity
15
Using the Weather

Name..

How much water do you use?

In the UK each person uses an average of 150 litres of water a day. Keep a tally to show how much water you use in one day.

	Number of times	Total litres
Having a bath – 90 litres		
Having a shower – 30 litres		
Brushing teeth – 1 litre		
A mug of tea or glass of squash – 0.25/¼ litre		
Washing hands – 3 litres		
Anything else you want to add?		

An average family uses these amounts per day: cooking – 12 litres; washing up – 12 litres; washing machine – 100 litres. Estimate your share of these amounts. Add them to the total.

Total

My share is

.... litres

Water is essential for life. We need to look after our water supply. Put some ideas to save water in the raindrops on this page.

FOG

World Weather

Using the temperature data banks, children can:

* Incorporate them in the activity sheet 'World weather chart' on page 26.

* Plot the cities and one week's temperatures on a world map.

* Compare these readings with a day in the present week. The Saturday *Daily Telegraph* is a good source.

* Plan a route on a world map, travelling from coldest to hottest location.

* Set up a database on a computer program such as 'Our Facts', and enter and use the figures to draw graphs and charts.

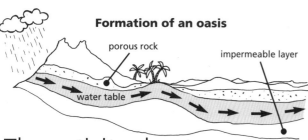

Formation of an oasis

porous rock

impermeable layer

water table

The activity sheets

16. Hot places

All life in the desert depends on water. Houses have flat roofs because there is no rain, white paint reflects the heat and verandahs provide shade. Wells are sunk to obtain water which is used to irrigate the land. Date palms provide a desert crop. Four-wheel drive vehicles are used to cross sand. The camel driver carries water, and a scarf to wrap around head and face to protect not only against the sun, but also against sandstorms. His flowing clothes help him to keep cool.

Questions to help children with the work:

* Why have jars been left under the date palm?
* What does the man hope the fence will do?
* How can you keep out of the sun in this village?

17. Cold places

In polar lands fishing is an important occupation. Fish are dried and smoked for storing and for export. Houses are built on stacks to allow for snow melting and ground movement. Transport is by vehicles with runners. Seals are mammals with large amounts of blubber to keep them warm. They build dens in the ice, entering from the water below. Their enemies are polar bears, who can slide silently into the water, and man. The Greenlander wears well-insulated clothes, often made from animal skins. He travels over the ice with huskies, a skidoo or a snowmobile. He carries a gun as protection against bears. Questions to help children with the work include:

* How can you keep fish without it going bad?
* Why are Greenlanders fishermen and not farmers?
* Why may frozen ground be unstable for building houses?

18. Tornadoes

Tornadoes are also called whirlwinds or twisters; over the sea they are called waterspouts. Their 200 m.p.h. winds devastate everything in their path. Differences in pressure in thunderclouds cause a vortex that acts like a vacuum cleaner, sucking things up and tossing them into the air. Tornadoes are common in central USA.

19a. World weather chart and 19b. Temperature data banks

Sheets 19A and 19B practise use and interpretation of data. Children can design symbols and create their own image of a place and its weather for the weather report.

Display idea

Use the charts for global awareness work, displaying the charts around a world map and joining them with rows of weather symbols or ribbons to their locations. Unhitch the ribbons to make the display interactive – children locate and match charts to the world map.

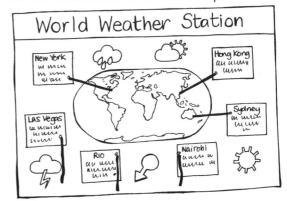

FOG

Name...

Hot places

Use this picture of an oasis to make a list of the ways people adapt to desert life. Make a drawing to show one of the ways you have listed. Write a caption for your picture.

The camel is a desert animal. Write a list of its features and explain how they help the camel to live in the desert. Draw the camel rider. Add labels to show how he adapts to desert life.

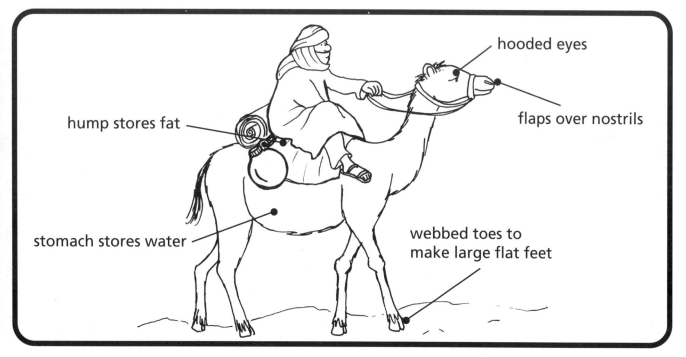

hooded eyes

flaps over nostrils

hump stores fat

stomach stores water

webbed toes to make large flat feet

FOG

Cold places

Use this picture of a harbour in Greenland to make a list of the ways people adapt to polar life. Make a drawing to show one of the ways in your list. Write a caption for your picture.

Seals live in cold water. Use the clues in the picture to write down some of the ways animals adapt to cold places. Draw the Greenlander. Add labels to explain what he wears and carries.

fur coat

pup in den under ice

blubber for warmth

steamlined shape for swimming

Tornadoes

This house had a television aerial, a tall chimney and a fence.

Outside was parked a car and a motor bike.

Three trees grew along the road.

Draw the things the tornado is tossing into the air or has smashed on to the ground.

Then, cover the vortex of the tornado and its thundercloud with dark paper.

Name...

World weather chart

Write the name of a city from the temperature data banks at the top of the chart. Find its location from an atlas and mark it on the small world map. Look at the temperature data banks to record four weeks of July weather.

.... weather station

Date	Temperature	Weather	

Decorate your chart with symbols or pictures connected with the weather or the city. Write a short report about your city's July weather, and add a symbol that tells at a glance what the weather has been like.

Weather report for ....

....

....

....

At a glance

FOG

Name..

Temperature data banks

Date: Saturday 4 July 1998		
City	°C	Weather
Athens	37	s
Bahrain	43	f
Buenos Aires	12	s
Cairo	34	s
Cape Town	13	c
Hong Kong	25	sh
London	19	c
New York	25	f
Reykjavik	11	r
Sydney	16	s

Date: Saturday 11 July 1998		
City	°C	Weather
Athens	29	s
Bahrain	42	s
Buenos Aires	15	s
Cairo	35	s
Cape Town	18	s
Hong Kong	31	f
London	21	f
New York	26	f
Reykjavik	12	r
Sydney	8	r

Date: Saturday 18 July 1998		
City	°C	Weather
Athens	32	s
Bahrain	41	s
Buenos Aires	14	r
Cairo	33	s
Cape Town	15	f
Hong Kong	32	f
London	22	r
New York	29	c
Reykjavik	15	f
Sydney	15	c

Date: Saturday 25 July 1998		
City	°C	Weather
Athens	36	s
Bahrain	45	s
Buenos Aires	16	c
Cairo	33	s
Cape Town	17	s
Hong Kong	33	c
London	21	s
New York	27	th
Reykjavik	10	c
Sydney	15	sh

Key: c=cloudy, f=fair, r=rain, s=sunny, sh=showers, th=thunder.

16

FOG

Effects of Weather

The activity sheets

20. When it rains
Children should understand the words 'evaporation' and 'condensation', the two physical processes that occur in the water cycle. The puddle activity is an example of evaporation. Condensation occurs when moist air cools, e.g. a child's breath misting up a mirror.

21. How the weather affects me
Start this activity with a class discussion on the way weather affects people. Share the ideas on the large symbols and then allow children to complete their personal sheet.

22. Wear-and-tear detective
Discuss with the class the damage done by different weather. Sun causes drying out, fading and blistering. Dark paint absorbs heat and will need repainting more often than white paint. The wind also causes drying out, it loosens and it erodes by carrying small particles. Rain washes away these loose particles, and causes rot. Icy weather causes a freeze-thaw effect which causes brickwork, stones and cement to crack. You may like to put out markers to indicate where children should look for weathering or mark locations for detective work on a school plan, turning the activity into a trail.

23. The weather and jobs
Ask a selection of employees in your school – caretaker, secretary, dinner supervisor, teacher, lollipop patrol – having a good spread of indoor and outdoor jobs. Extend it for local area work, e.g. shopkeepers who keep seasonal stock, people who wear seasonal uniforms, caterers and transport workers.

24. Using the survey data
It is important that children understand the need to read and make conclusions from survey data (see example).

Season: Spring		In spring I sell more chocolate for Easter and Mother's Day.
Weather		When it rains people make the shop muddy.
Travel		Once I had an accident and the shop was closed until noon.

25. London Transport
In the late 1920s, London Transport created many posters to encourage people to get out and about whatever the weather. Posters and postcards of them are available from the London Transport Museum, Convent Garden Piazza, London WC2E 7BB. Tel: 0171 379 6344. The air of London, people were told, was clouded and heavy with smoke. The public were encouraged to escape to the country by bus, and 'swap the smoke for the sunshine'.

26. Winter transport hazards
In Canada, roads can be isolated and exposed. Ditches on roadsides are made to clear snow into, but can be a danger for cars which skid off the road. Lack of hedges makes the edge of the road difficult to see after snow.

27. Avalanche!
An avalanche is sliding snow that carries boulders and rocks, can reach speeds of 100 m.p.h. and freezes like concrete when it stops. It occurs when fresh, loose snow, easy to dig, like sugar crystals, lies on top of a compacted layer; it is easily dislodged by vibrations.

Display idea
Use large weather symbols, as in Activity 21, to make a large class collage of one weather type. Umbrella shapes made of shiny paper work well and make a dramatic display mounted on dark paper with grey raindrops. Large umbrella shapes, which can be lifted up, can shelter poems or stories related to the weather.

When it rains...

dark background

window catch

felt tip on border, splashed with water to make it run

16

22

FOG

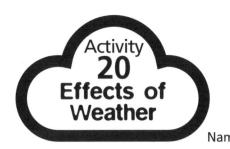

Activity
20
Effects of Weather

Name..

When it rains

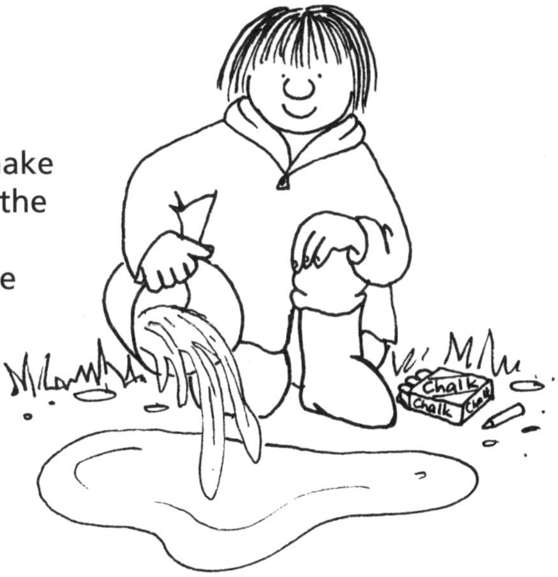
Chalk
Chalk

Puddles. No rain? Use a bucket of water to make your own puddle! Use chalk to draw around the puddle, close to the water's edge. Revisit the puddle at intervals, and draw the next outline as the puddle gradually gets smaller.

What is happening to the water?
Where is it going?

Follow that raindrop!
Some raindrops evaporate from surface water into the air. Most take longer to become water vapour in the water cycle. The diagram shows you how water circulates in the environment.

Fill in the blank spaces.

Heat from the sun .... sea water.

It becomes water ....

As it rises it cools and forms ....

As it cools more the water vapour ....

It .... on the hills.

The water finds its way to a ....

It flows downhill to the ....

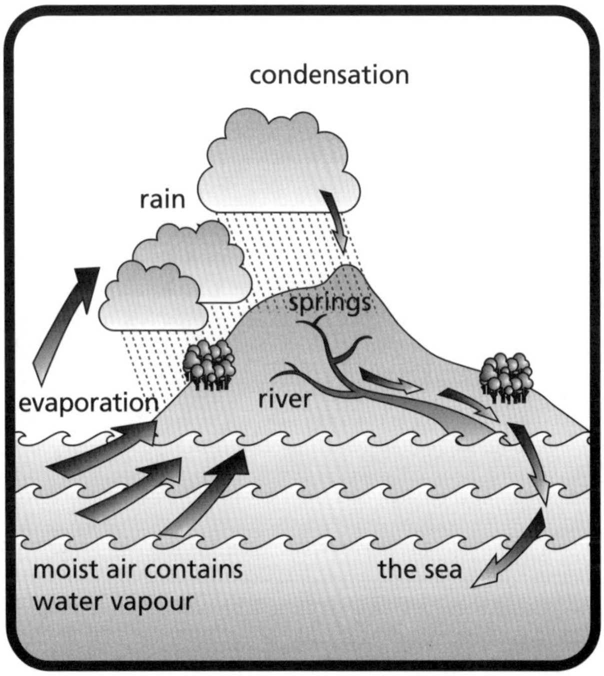
condensation
rain
springs
evaporation
river
moist air contains
water vapour
the sea

Trace the passage of a raindrop in your area.
Use a local map to discover which stream or river it finds. Trace its journey to the sea. Make a simple map to show its route.

How the weather affects me

These shapes represent different weather. In each shape write the answer to one of the following questions.

✸ How does this sort of weather make you feel?
✸ What do you wear?
✸ What do you like doing in this weather?
✸ What does this weather stop you from doing?
✸ What things do you notice when the weather is like this?

If you trace the weather symbol and cut out a matching shape, you can make a decorated flap for your weather thoughts, like the umbrella shown here.

© 1998 Channel Four Learning Limited

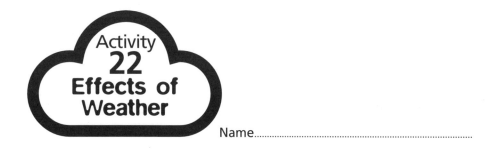
Wear-and-tear detective

The weather has damaged your school.
Look around for everyday weathering in your school grounds.
Tick the boxes if you find evidence.

Paintwork

☐ faded?
☐ blistered?
☐ peeling?

Bricks

☐ loosened mortar?
☐ chips and cracks?
☐ worn edges?

Tarmac

☐ uneven?
☐ cracks?
☐ loose stones?

Windows

☐ draughty?
☐ putty cracked?
☐ frames rotten?

Fences

☐ panels loose?
☐ posts rotten and
  wobbly?
☐ wood dry and faded?

Try to work out if it was the weather, and what sort of weather
caused the damage. Make a report on one area of weathering you
have noticed. Answer these questions in your report.
* Where is it?
* What is it like?
* What caused it?
* Can it be repaired?

Sketch of the damage	Weathering report

FOG

Name..

The weather and jobs

You can use this survey sheet to find out how the weather affects a person's job. You may be able to ask the questions directly, or you may need to leave the sheet with them. Can you guess what some of the answers may be?

The weather and your job

Can you help me to find out how the weather affects different people's jobs by answering these questions.

1. What is your job? ....

2. Do you work indoors/outdoors? ....

3. Do you do different work in different seasons? Yes/no. If 'yes', please explain.

In spring ....   In summer ....

In autumn ....   In winter ....

4. How does each sort of weather affect your job?

Rain ....

Fog ....

Snow ....

Hot temperatures ....

5. How do you usually travel to work? ....

6. Has the weather ever had an effect on your journey? Yes/no. If 'yes', please explain.

....

Thank you for helping with the survey.

FOG

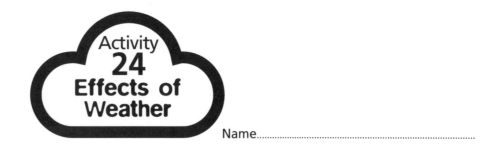

Name..

Using the survey data

How does the weather affect a person's job?
Draw a symbol or picture in the pictorial report boxes, and explain the effect of the
weather in the written report. Choose the most interesting season and weather type from
your survey sheet to fill in your report.

Job ....

Pictorial report	Written report
Season	
Weather	
Travel	

How much effect does the weather have on this job?

Conclusion ....

....

FOG

London Transport

Seventy years ago, in the early days of the London Underground, posters with slogans about the weather encouraged people to use the 'Tube'.

Choose one of the slogans and design your own advert for travel on the tube.

**The underground's the only spot
For comfort when the days are hot.**

**Cold rain and fog on top abound
Descend to brightness underground.**

Think about the images you can create for the weather in London and the comfort offered by travel underground.

FOG

Name..

Winter transport hazards

From a Canadian child's school diary.

25 October
Mom has put her winter gear in the trunk
of the car. There's a shovel, a broom, a foil
blanket, some chocolate and a mobile
phone. She calls them her lifesavers. Why
has she packed each item?

....

....

....

....

....

....

....

....

....

....

....

....

....

....

....

As the newspaper's photographer, make a sketch to show the photo you will take to show one of the problems in the city.

Give your photograph a caption.

The Evening News

Weather causes transport problems

Severe winter weather has caused problems with the city's transport. Cars, buses, taxis, trains and planes have all had problems getting people to work.

FOG

Avalanche!

Add pictures to illustrate this
avalanche adventure.

Fresh snow fell on the mountain. The
sun is shining and all the skiers are out.
Two men with snowmobiles go up to
the high, empty slopes.

Their engine vibrations start a slide of
snow. They try to race ahead of the
avalanche as it roars behind them at 100
m.p.h. The avalanche overtakes them.

They are buried deep in the snow.
Rescuers dig quickly. The snow is
unstable and may move. It is very cold.
The men are lucky to be alive.

Put captions in the 'bubbles' to
show what the different people
thought about the avalanche.

FOG

Weatherproof Design

The activities in this section link with work in science and design technology, giving an opportunity to develop and test an idea.

The albedo effect

Black absorbs heat and white reflects it, hence white houses in hot countries and black solar bags for yacht deck showers. Place thermometers under a black umbrella and a white one on a sunny day and note the difference in the temperature readings.

Insulation

Some materials insulate better than others. Try wrapping jars of hot water in scarves of different materials. At the beginning of the investigation and then every half hour, take the temperature of the water and compare results.

Waterproofing

Plant labels for the garden can be written in different inks and tested on rainy days for waterproof capability. This can lead to designing plant labels that will be waterproof, using materials available in the classroom.

The activity sheets

28. Sun-seekers

The experiment introduces the children to the albedo effect of different colours reflecting or absorbing heat from the sun. It is best to use small bottles, say 500 ml, and wrap them tightly with dustbin liners or carrier bags; fix around the rim with clear tape. The bottles should have tops to prevent loss of heat. The difference in temperature readings are seen within half an hour. It may take longer if the sun is not very strong. Following the results, children can design a coloured sunshade that will reflect rather than absorb heat. How much heat will they allow to be absorbed in order to have the colour of their choice? Was it a fair test? Were there similarities in size of bottle, amount of water, thickness of plastic covering?

29. Santa's no-skidoo

A design activity sheet to produce an all-weather multi-terrain vehicle for delivery of Christmas presents. Children may need to be taught that tyres have treads to create friction so that cars do not slide on the road. Vehicles used on snow and ice have a large contact surface in order to spread the weight so the vehicle does not sink.

30. 'Which weather' quiz

Display idea

Make a display table of items that the children bring in or make that have good weatherproofing. Make logos for The Weatherproof Design Company on self-adhesive labels to award to items that the children present and recommend as having good weatherproof features. Start them off with an example, a coolbox or a windbreak perhaps.

FOG

Name..

Sun-seekers

In sunny places, sailors hang special bags of water, called solar bags, on deck all day to heat in the sun. In the evening they use the solar bags to take a warm shower on deck.
What colour bag will produce the warmest shower?
This experiment will help you to find out.

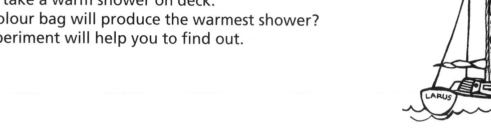

1. Take three plastic bottles with lids. Cover them tightly with different coloured plastic bags – black, white and your favourite colour.
2. Fill the bottles with water, leave them in the sun and take the temperature of each every half hour.
3. Fill in the table opposite.

Colour	
Black	.... °C
White	.... °C
My colour is	
....	.... °C

Which bottle had the warmest water?
What have you learnt about heat from the sun on different colours?
Design a sunshade for the people on the boat. What colour will it be?

Name...

Santa's no-skidoo

Was Santa late getting to you last year, or were you one of the lucky ones?

Following the accident to his sleigh, a new all-weather, multi-terrain vehicle is needed for next Christmas to get all the presents delivered on time.

Make some notes below.

The worst weather he might meet ....

Vehicle features needed for:

Rain .... Sun ....

Snow .... Fog ....

Types of terrain to cross ....

Time of day for travel ....

Food and drink for journey ....

....

Safety equipment ....

....

Draw and label your idea for a vehicle that will do the job next Christmas and get the stockings filled on time.

Name...

'Which weather?' quiz

The weather has caused some curious things to happen.

Word clues:

sun   evaporation   prevailing wind   erosion   loss of friction   rain
knock-on effect   wind   temperature   sandstorm   burst   hurricane

Match two words or phrases to each picture.
Add a caption that explains what has happened.

....

....

....

....

....

....

....

....

....

....

....

....

Choose one of the pictures. Draw your own picture showing how people are affected by this weather condition.

FOG